Emergency Poems

Compiled by John Foster

OXFORD

Oxford University Press, Walton Street, Oxford, OX2 6DP

Oxford New York Toronto
Delhi Bombay Calcutta Madras Karachi
Kuala Lumpur Singapore Hong Kong Tokyo
Nairobi Dar es Salaam Cape Town
Melbourne Auckland Madrid

and associated companies in
Berlin Ibadan

Oxford is a trade mark of Oxford University Press

Acknowledgements
The Editor and Publisher wish to thank the following who have kindly
given their permission for the use of copyright material:

Eric Finney for 'Tree emergency' © 1993 Eric Finney; John Foster for
'Lost and found' and 'Lifeboat rescue' both © 1993 John Foster;
Tony Mitton for 'Fire in the night' and 'Emergencies' both © 1993
Tony Mitton; Jill Townsend for 'Night arrival' © 1993 Jill Townsend;
Celia Warren for 'Blue flashing light' © 1993 Celia Warren.

Although every effort has been made to contact the owners of
copyright material, a few have been impossible to trace, but if they
contact the Publisher, correct acknowledgement will be made in
future editions.

Illustrations by
Shelagh McNicholas   Ann Johns
Bethan Matthews   Zoe Pearson
  Lewis

Fire in the night

What's that crackling?
Fire in the night!
Leaping flames
and orange light.

Pick up the telephone:
999.
Firemen hurry.
Sirens whine.

Here comes the engine,
rumbling and red,
blue light flashing
on its grumbling head.

Out jump the firemen.
'Back!' they shout.
'Bring on the hoses.
Put the blaze out.'

Tony Mitton

Lost and found

'If you're lost,' said Mum,
'What you must do
Is ask the police
And they'll help you.'

Last night, we were walking
Through the fun fair.
When I looked round
Mum and Dad weren't there.

So I asked a policewoman
What I should do
And she said, 'Don't worry,
I'll find them for you.'

As we walked along,
She held my hand.
Then we went in a van
By the hot-dog stand.

6

She told me to sit
And wait in a chair,
Then suddenly
Mum and Dad were there!

So if you get lost,
What you must do
Is ask the police
And they'll help you.

John Foster

7

Blue flashing light

On the top of an ambulance
A blue flashing light
Travels like a shooting star
Fast through the night.

Here is an emergency,
Somewhere someone's ill,
The blue star is rushing
While the night stands still.

Celia Warren

9

Emergencies

Red alert!
Red alert!
I've dropped my lolly
in the dirt.

SOS
SOS
I've spilt some custard
down my dress.

999
999
I've ridden my bike
through the washing-line.

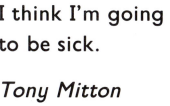

Ambulance,
and make it quick!
I think I'm going
to be sick.

Tony Mitton

Tree emergency

Emergency! Emergency!
Our Jamie's gone and
Got stuck up a tree.
We lifted him up
To get the ball,
Now we've got that back
But he can't move at all.
Get on the phone quick,
Emergency!
Fire, Police, Ambulance—
We'll need all three.

How high up is he?
Well, not very high.
We could reach him
From the garden chair.
Why don't we try?
Rescue party quick!
I'll show you how.
He might have got down
On his own by now.

Eric Finney

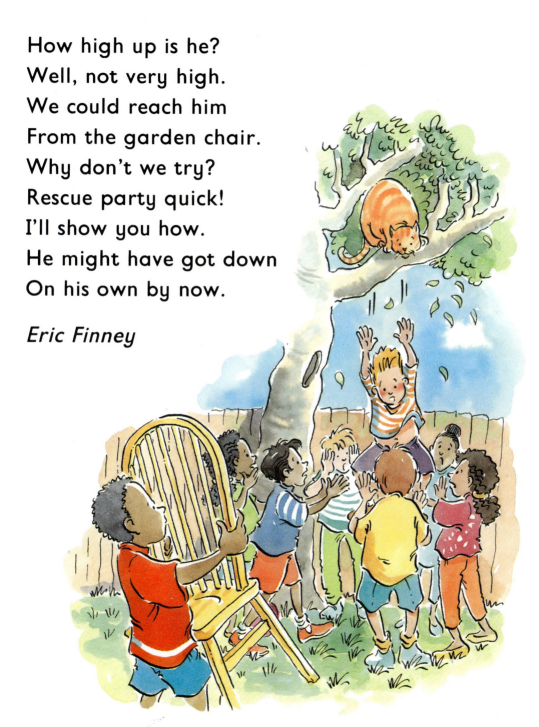

Lifeboat rescue

The waves are huge.
There's a howling gale.
The tiny boat
Has lost its sail.

The coastguard
Spots the tiny boat,
Sees a girl struggling
To keep it afloat.

He sounds the alarm.
Emergency!
The lifeboat sets off
Across the sea.

The huge waves try
To block its way.
But the lifeboat hurries
Across the bay.

The girl is rescued,
And once again
A life is saved
By the lifeboatmen.

John Foster

Night arrival

The ambulance was white.
It came the other night
and took my mum away.

We saw her the next day
with a grin a mile wide
and a baby by her side.

Jill Townsend